Runtie and Tudi's
Grand Sailing Adventure
A True Story

Sharon Stevens-Smith
Illustrated by Alfred Galaroza

Runtie and Tudie's Grand Sailing Adventure
Copyright © 2023 by Sharon Stevens-Smith

All rights reserved. No part of this publication may be reproduced, distributed, or transmitted in any form or by any means, including photocopying, recording, or other electronic or mechanical methods, without the prior written permission of the author, except in the case of brief quotations embodied in critical reviews and certain other non-commercial uses permitted by copyright law.

Tellwell Talent
www.tellwell.ca

ISBN
978-0-2288-9169-7 (Hardcover)
978-0-2288-9170-3 (Paperback)
978-1-7794-1525-7 (eBook)

For Ricky, Bradyn,
Rylee and Maddie

INTRODUCTION

This is the captivating true story of two Calico cats, Tudie and Runtie, whose extraordinary courage and remarkable adaptability propelled them on an amazing ocean voyage. They set sail from the shores of Victoria, British Columbia, Canada, along with their Mistress and Captain, embarking on an amazing adventure that would span several years.

Tudie, a wise and motherly cat, had earned her name after being rescued as a tiny mewing kitten behind the old Tudor House Pub in Esquimalt, B.C. Her beautiful Calico fur shone with a magnificent blend of colors – orange, black and white.

Runtie, Tudie's timid yet resilient daughter, had been bestowed her name because she was the smallest of seven kittens. Though her colors were slightly more muted, they held a unique beauty that was equally as enchanting.

Their Mistress encountered an opportunity to embark on an offshore sailing expedition, but was unable to find Tudie and Runtie a new home. With a mixture of reluctance and determination, she took them along on this seafaring adventure.

This heartwarming story of Tudie and Runtie's magical journey, from the marinas to the open seas, reminds us all of the transformative power of embracing the unfamiliar, the depths of our own courage, the innate ability to adapt and the unbreakable strength of familial bonds.

Runtie and Tudie were Calico cats
Whose days in the sun were spent searching for rats.

Whirling and leaping, not a care in the world
Napping together, around each other they curled.

Mother and Daughter they were, such a strong bond
Always together from dusk until dawn.

Whispers they heard, day after day
Their Mistress made plans, "An adventure," she'd say.

Off to sea she would go, and many a year it would take
New plans for Runtie and Tudie,
their Mistress would make.

Oh no! She couldn't take cats, for
they would never survive
A new owner she'd find; on land they would thrive!

An ad was placed with photos so sweet
To find a new home and kind people to meet.

Alas, no home was found, so to her dismay
A sailing boat was where Runtie and Tudie would stay.

To the marina they went, a week it would be
Preparing the ship for adventures at sea.

Their food and beds and toys were all packed
Then loaded aboard in little brown sacks.

Tiny nooks and crannies on board did they find
For the Captain looked mean, but was ever so kind.

Their favourite places to sit were two bean bag chairs
Perched high on the deck, bringing curious stares.

Runtie was so timid; she rarely ventured out
Hiding on board, for safety did she scout.

Tudie wasn't shy; she explored the marina docks
Walking with care on floats that would rock.

One day, a mewing was heard as Tudie was called
Soaked to the skin, to a fish boat she had crawled.

Rescued at last; in a towel she was wrapped
Back to the boat, warm milk it was lapped.

Tudie grew restless exploring the marina docks
Until one lucky day, she spied a little red fox.

Running and leaping, the fun had begun
Enjoying the chase in the noonday sun.

Suddenly lost in a culvert, deep in a hole
Mewing was heard by a guard on patrol.

With flashlights, they searched late into the night
Until they found Tudie lodged down in a pipe.

Her nine lives were now at the number of eight
This adventuresome cat had crept through a grate.

Leaving land behind, they watched the setting sun
To warmer places, their journey had just begun.

Off to Mexico, they sailed with sea legs they found
Far, far from land; to the sea they were bound.

The sea was rough, and it rolled through the night
Runtie and Tudie hung on, their eyes wide with fright.

To the Captain's cabin they went, kitty litter and all
Going overboard now? Such a terrible fall!

The door was taped and sealed all around
As the boat swayed and lurched,
they heard a terrible sound.

For the wind was a-howl and the boat was a-heave
And the sails were a-snap; there seemed no reprieve.

Then the sea turned to calm, and
the wind settled down
Allowed up on deck, they strolled merrily around.

Flying through the air came fish from the sea
Landing on deck for Runtie and Tudie to see.

The dolphins rode on the waves at the bow
And sting rays soared grandly with wings oh so proud.

Two yellow birds, far from land did they search
For a plant on the ship, so tired did they perch.

In the Sea of Cortez, the boat it did sway
On Sundays came families in small boats for the day.

Round and round they circled to have a close look
Shouting and waving and photos they took.

Tudie was held high for the children to see
"Gato gordo!" they shouted as they pointed with glee.

For never a cat on the sea had they seen
Especially one with fur of such sheen.

Runtie loved to go fishing—at least she would try
Swatting at lures that were cast on the fly.

From the seas came the cats' dinner, each day a delight
As they dined on fresh fish with colours so bright.

Full of protein, their meals were caught every morn
For no luckier cats had ever been born!

Their Mistress was proud; so brave were her cats
Overcoming fears, being able to adapt!

How they loved the sea with its beautiful smells
As the waves pushed them onward
with slow, gentle swells.

And now they are known to the world far and wide
As two Calico cats who set sail with the tide.

SHARON STEVENS-SMITH

Raised on beautiful Vancouver Island surrounded by the vast Pacific Ocean, Sharon developed a fascination and deep respect for the ocean at a very early age.

This is the true story of this adventuresome woman who was unable to rehome her two Calico cats, named Runtie and Tudie, then reluctantly took them with her to sail offshore on an amazing adventure that was to span a number of years.

Calico cats are considered to bring good luck and fortune and are also considered to be a little magical because of their tri colors of black, orange and white. All of this was deemed to be true on their incredible ocean sailing journey.

Sharon's life of adventure has included studies of the diverse cultures and wildlife in Eastern Africa and assisting in observation and research of Orangutans on the Island of Borneo in Indonesia.

Aside from her experiences, Sharon is also a talented artist and avid gardener. Through it all she remains grounded and dedicated to living a meaningful life. Whether sailing the open ocean or tending to her garden, Sharon remains a force to be reckoned with, living life on her own terms and inspiring others to do the same.

Manufactured by Amazon.ca
Bolton, ON